Ove Arup & Partners

1 9 4 6 – 1 9 8 6

2

Ove Arup & Partners

1 9 4 6 – 1 9 8 6

ACADEMY EDITIONS · LONDON / ST. MARTIN'S PRESS · NEW YORK

First published in Great Britain in 1986 by
ACADEMY EDITIONS, 7 Holland Street, London W8

ISBN 0-85670-898-4

Published in the United States of America in 1986 by
ST. MARTIN'S PRESS, 175 Fifth Avenue, New York 10010

Library of Congress Catalog Card Number 86-042919
ISBN 0-312-00094-4

Printed and bound in Hong Kong

COVER
SYDNEY OPERA HOUSE
Australia

FRONTISPIECE
THE HONGKONG BANK
Hong Kong

TITLE PAGE
PENGUIN POOL
Zoological Gardens, London

On the occasion of the 40th anniversary of the founding of our firm we have published this volume illustrating some of the projects with which we have been concerned as Consulting Engineers, either in collaboration with architects or as principal designers in a prime agency capacity.

Ove Arup's philosophies of design have had an important influence on the development of our practice. Good building is derived from a synthesis of art, technology and the construction process. The engineer should not only be a master in his own field, but must also be able to appreciate and share the objectives and aspirations of other participants in the design and construction process – a tall order, but something to strive for.

The projects illustrated have been selected to give some impression of the breadth of skills within the practice, the nature of commissions undertaken and their location throughout the world. The selection of visual material which illustrates the art of engineering is challenging because it is not obvious except in a few buildings and in most bridges, where it is clearly expressed for all to see. Moreover, some of our early, interesting and pioneering projects were not as lovingly visually recorded as our most recent work.

Although the practice is very large it is still committed to the original ideals of Arup himself, a belief in the social purpose of design, the pursuit of excellence and the holistic nature of the design and construction process.

PATSCENTER
Princeton, USA

HIGHPOINT
Highgate, London

‘Engineering is not a science. Science studies particular events to find general laws. Engineering design makes use of these laws to solve particular problems. In this it is more closely related to art or craft; as in art, its problems are under-defined, there are many solutions, good, bad or indifferent. The art is, by a synthesis of ends and means, to arrive at a good solution. This is a creative activity, involving imagination, intuition and deliberate choice.’

Ove Arup

Bovis

PROJECTS 1946 – 1986

Rationalisation of the building process to solve the immediate post-war housing crisis. Designed for a 10 year life, of the thousands erected many are still occupied today.

An early application of the reinforced concrete wall and slab 'box frame' construction.

The commencement of the firm's first overseas practice.

RUBBER FACTORY
Brynmawr, Wales

The practice's first shell roof design.

FOOTBRIDGE
Festival of Britain, London

A prestressed, post-tensioned cast in situ concrete structure with four spans of 16m to 22m.

This was the first total design undertaken by the Building Group of the partnership. Its success, together with other commissions which followed, led to the formation of Arup Associates in 1964.

A simple structure of welded tubular steel three-pinned space frames.

An early application of years of research into the plastic behaviour of steel frames.

BANK OF ENGLAND PRINTING WORKS
Debden, Essex

27m span prestressed concrete arches and shell roofs.

A barrel vault shell roof, prestressed to obviate a waterproof membrane.

One of the partnership's first projects with London County Council's Housing Division.

The structure included a shallow prismatic tubular steel diagrid roof over the conference hall.

Prestressed concrete shell roofs cast at ground level and jacked into position via their supporting blockwork columns.

PRINCESS MARGARET HOSPITAL
Swindon, Wiltshire

PARK HILL HOUSING
Sheffield, Yorkshire

The partnership's first reinforced concrete telecommunication towers 240m and 269m high respectively.

26 ST JAMES'S PLACE
London

The nave canopy is comprised of a tracery of slender precast, prestressed concrete beams supported by thin columns formed from precast, prestressed concrete elements.

Projects which resulted in the partnership establishing a permanent presence in West Africa from 1951.

A labour-intensive rationalised method of construction and the beginning of the firm's presence in East Africa.

A 69m x 39m x 9m high elliptical paraboloid concrete shell roof, larger and flatter than any such dome previously built.

When constructed, this 26 storey block was by far the tallest in Lagos.

A bridge cast in two similar sections parallel with each bank and swivelled to meet over the river.

DUNELM HOUSE
Durham University

HAMPSTEAD CIVIC CENTRE
London

Precision in precast concrete.

NINEWELLS HOSPITAL
Dundee, Scotland

FAIRYDEAN FOOTBALL CLUB STAND
Galashiels, Scotland

NO
ENTRY
NO PARKING

AHMADU BELLO STADIUM
Kaduna, Nigeria

Reinforced concrete shell roofs were economical at the time for industrial buildings in Africa.

ASSEMBLY HALL
Bootham School, York

A structural steel access tower designed as part of improvements to the hostel.

Precast, prestressed Y-shaped roof beams fabricated at ground level and lifted into position between their supporting columns.

VOLTA RIVER BRIDGES
Ghana

SAPELE BRIDGES
Nigeria

Early river bridges in West Africa.

TERMINAL BUILDING
Abbotsinch Airport, Glasgow

A 50m high tower constructed in precast concrete: three leg units, a mast and an interconnecting key element.

Physics Building

Falmer House

Brick-clad reinforced concrete frames utilizing thin precast concrete barrel vault ceiling units – a theme repeated through most buildings on the campus.

A suspended structure in reinforced and prestressed concrete.

ROYAL COMMONWEALTH POOL
Edinburgh

Twin road bridges with quadrupedal central supports, enabling the two parts of the University campus to be connected via a pedestrian concourse.

The partnership has been responsible for the design and supervision of over 3,500km of trunk, feeder and suburban roads and their associated bridges, culverts and other works.

P

Barber-Greene

RAISING AND REFURBISHING THE WELLINGTON INN
Market Place, Manchester

The inn, built *circa* 1462, is scheduled as an ancient monument. Its retention was essential within the new development, but this necessitated raising the building 1.46m. This was achieved by first underpinning, and then jacking, into its final position.

A two level road system through the centre of Gateshead. The form of the viaduct structure allows the slip road ramps to merge in gradually.

The 8½km by-pass with its associated interchanges and bridges was the first of the partnership's many motorway type projects in the UK.

The Crucible Theatre
The Crucible Theatre

Designed, constructed and operational within two years. When built, the 328m concrete tower was the tallest in the UK and the third highest structure of its type in the world.

THE STOCK EXCHANGE
London

ALMONDELL FOOTBRIDGE
Scotland

BERNAT KLEIN STUDIO
High Sunderland, Scotland

A Gothic cathedral rising from Roman, Saxon and Norman foundations, requiring 20th-century technology to arrest further structural deformation.

A very high standard of finishes, integration of all services and rapid commissioning were prime requirements for the planning, design and construction of this large, complex brewery.

EFN 61L

A mullioned elevation expressing the load carried.

SOCIETY OF FRIENDS MEETING HOUSE
Blackheath, London

The 39m square, two layer, steel space frame roof over the conference hall is supported by only four columns.

The horizontal distribution of services is integrated within the four 36m x 30m Nodus space frames of the warehouse and the 30m square space frame over the showroom.

A structural form determined by analysing a hanging chain model and inverting the result. The roof structures are fabricated from grids of timber struts laid horizontally and jacked into position.

The conference halls and seminar rooms resembling Bedouin tents are aluminium-clad, cable-stayed structures.

BISHOPTHORPE BRIDGE
York

The partnership's first major road project in the Far East. A 200km trunk and feeder road network through primary jungle.

Several hundred steel lattice communication towers and guyed masts have been built in over 20 countries. Major projects have included telecommunication networks in Nigeria, Bolivia, Chile and Ireland.

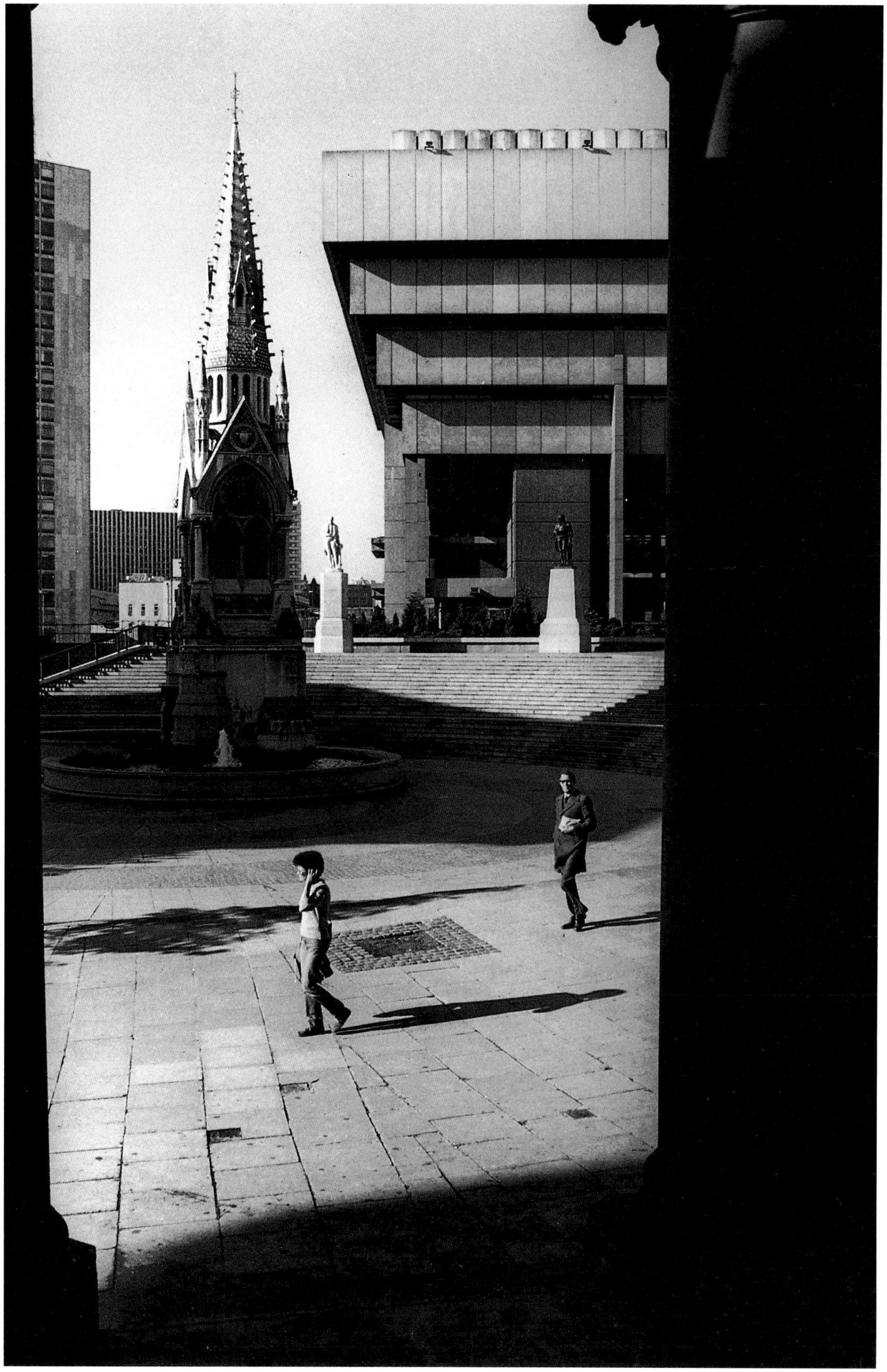

BERRY LANE VIADUCT
M25, Hertfordshire

The viaduct carries the six lane M25 across a pleasant wooded valley. The impact on its surroundings has been reduced as much as possible by the structural form of the bridge deck – supported on slender circular concrete columns.

A 'theatre in the round' inside Manchester's Edwardian Cotton Exchange. As the original floor could not carry its entire weight, deep tubular steel trusses span 30m between piers to support the galleries and roof.

SIAK RIVER BRIDGE
Sumatra, Indonesia

LIBRARY
St Andrew's University, Scotland

ICE CAPADES
WE REACH THE MOON
MOON SITE
PUBLIC SCULPTURE URBAN ENVIRONMENT
great
architecture in chicago

RUNNYMEDE BRIDGE
M25, near Staines

This, together with an earlier adjacent bridge designed by Lutyens, carries the M25 motorway over the River Thames. It reflects the form of the older structure but belongs to its own time. White concrete frames were cast in halves on the banks, slid into position and connected at mid-span.

The 815m long viaduct carries the Tyne & Wear Metro over the Ouseburn Valley. It was the first bridge in the UK to be built by cantilever construction from precast, prestressed concrete segments with glued joints.

The interchange relieves congestion on the main road along the north coast of Wales. Landscaped earth mounds soften its presence and shield the local community from traffic.

The partnership was responsible for all structures within the sea wall together with access roads and ramps.

The redevelopment of Telford's Dock and the restoration of Hardwick's warehouses. One of the first projects to bring new life to London's derelict docklands.

DICKENS INN

IRONSIDES
WILL

Rising 215m above street level, the circular building is the tallest concrete structure in Hong Kong. Situated on a steep granite slope, its main entrance is located some 55m above the lower boundary. Extensive drainage and rock anchors were necessary to ensure stability of the structure.

BRENT C FLARE TOWER
North Sea

A 100m high flare tower which involved one of the highest offshore lifts in the world.

HUTTON TENSION LEG PLATFORM
North Sea

The world's first tension leg oil production platform, for which specialist engineering and management services were supplied.

The tensile structure of Hall 7 provides for 10,000m^2 of floor space free from vertical supports.

RESTORATION OF THEATRE ROYAL AND NEW CONCERT HALL
Nottingham

In addition to the restoration of the theatre, the project included the construction of a new, fully air-conditioned 2,500 seat concert hall.

AULD BRIG O'DOON
Strathclyde, Scotland

Restoration of this famous stone bridge built *circa* 1450.

ROBINSON COLLEGE
Cambridge University

PRINCE PHILIP DENTAL TEACHING HOSPITAL
Hong Kong

CARLSBERG BREWERY
Hong Kong
A brewery constructed for the most part on reclaimed ground.

ASHLEY CENTRE
Epsom, Surrey

THE FRIARY CENTRE
Guildford, Surrey

FLEETGUARD FACTORY AND DISTRIBUTION CENTRE
Quimper, France

One of the partnership's first cable-stayed roofs.

THE BARBICAN REDEVELOPMENT
London

Accommodation for 6,000 people in a development which includes the tallest residential buildings in London. The subterranean Arts Centre required advanced structural and geotechnical analysis for its realisation.

The roof structure is designed to accommodate distribution of the comprehensive services requirement.

The partnership's first project of this type in the Middle East.

An industrial plant in the attractive setting of the Southern Highlands of New South Wales.

Conversion of an old industrial structure into housing accommodation.

ALLENDALE SQUARE
Perth, Australia

A loading facility for 80,000-ton oil tankers. Its cylindrical shaft anchored to the sea bed was the first to be constructed of prestressed concrete.

ARTICULATED LOADING COLUMN
Maureen Field, North Sea

Luk Yeung Sun Chuen Development

One of several projects for the Mass Transit in Hong Kong, the Tsuen Wan Depot includes a maintenance depot, sidings and a station under a development housing some 25,000 people.

Tsuen Wan Depot

The refurbishment of a 1,100 seat auditorium and upgrading of the stage area to accommodate large musical productions.

THEATRE ROYAL
Plymouth

A highly serviced refurbishment of an existing office block with the provision of a new atrium.

RENAULT CENTRE
Swindon, Wiltshire

The curved alignment of the bridge with a main span of 132m fits the road closely into the rocky landscape.

This 600m^2 PTFE coated-glass fabric membrane canopy provides a permanent roof to cover an open-air theatre.

NEW GRANDSTAND
Lansdowne Road, Dublin

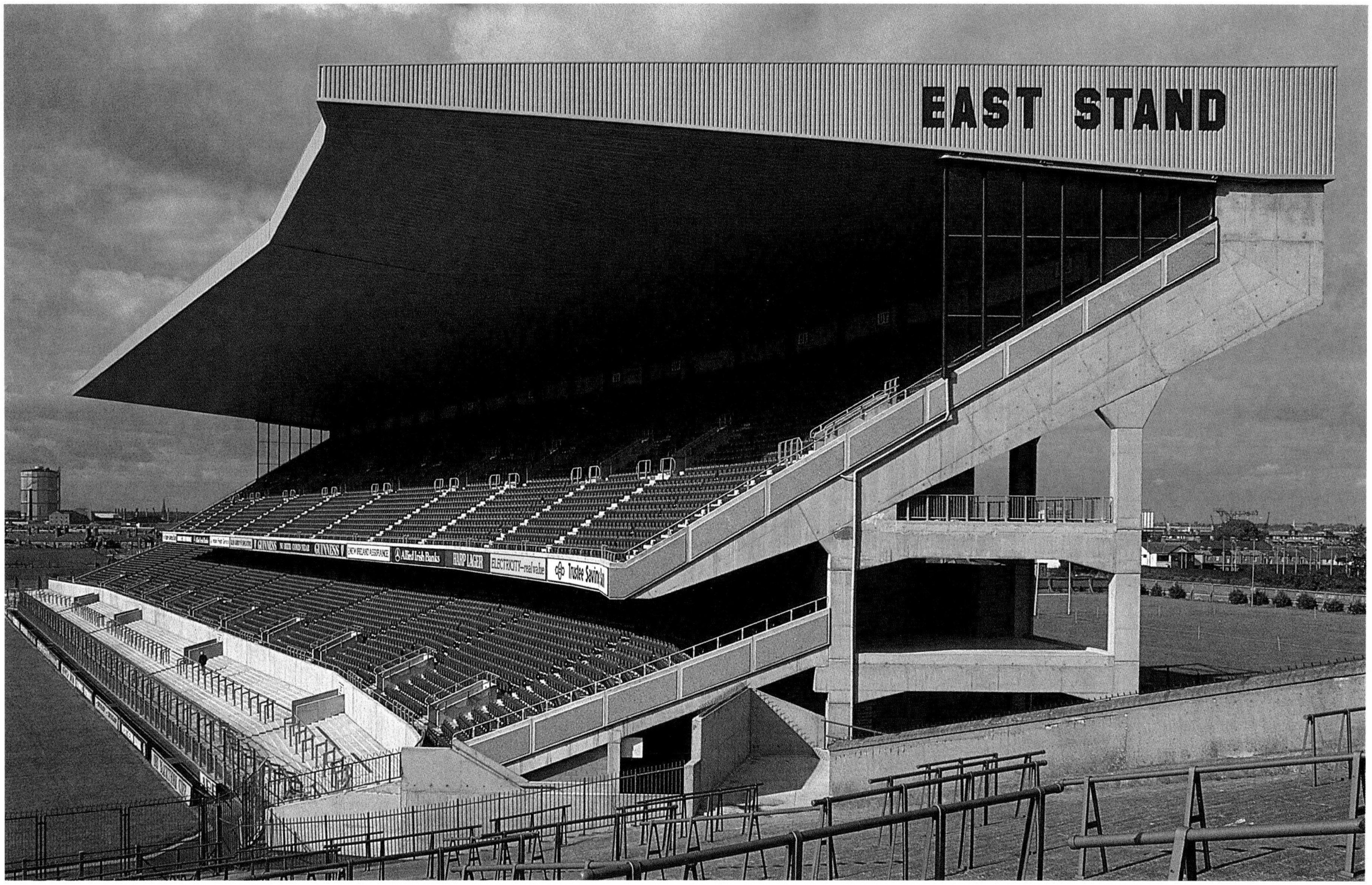

A 670km dual three lane motorway, including 100 bridges, interchanges and 100km of feeder roads.

QATAR UNIVERSITY
Doha, Qatar

This 40km length of motorway between the M5 and M6 was aligned specifically to affect as few properties as possible. The project includes 67 bridges, 7 junctions with trunk roads, and full connections to the adjoining motorways.

FITTING OUT PROJECTS

Modern work stations with all their complex information technology equipment require very highly serviced buildings. The design of fully integrated service systems to support such offices is one of the specialist skills within the partnership.

Atlas House, London

I Finsbury Avenue, London

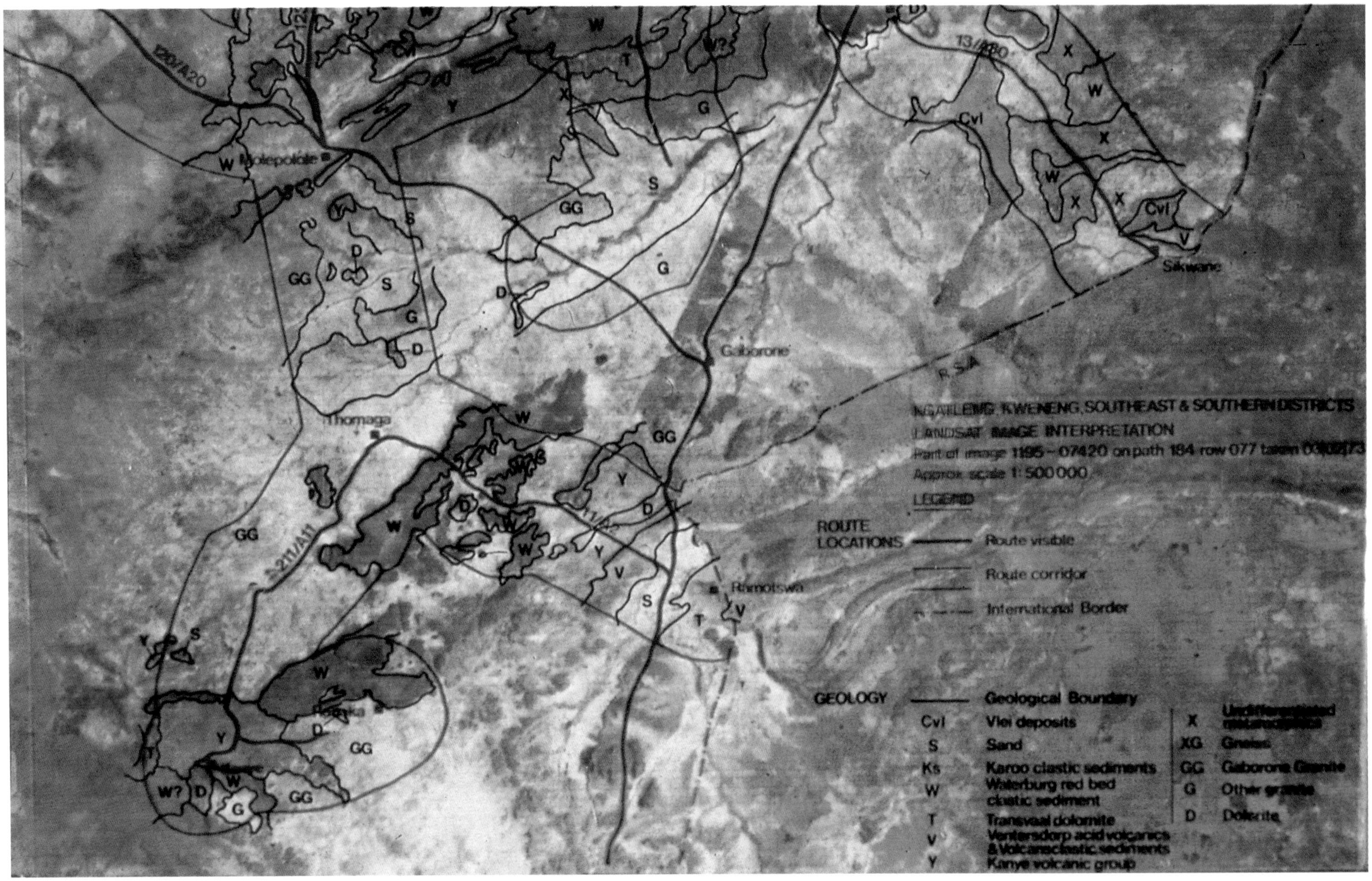

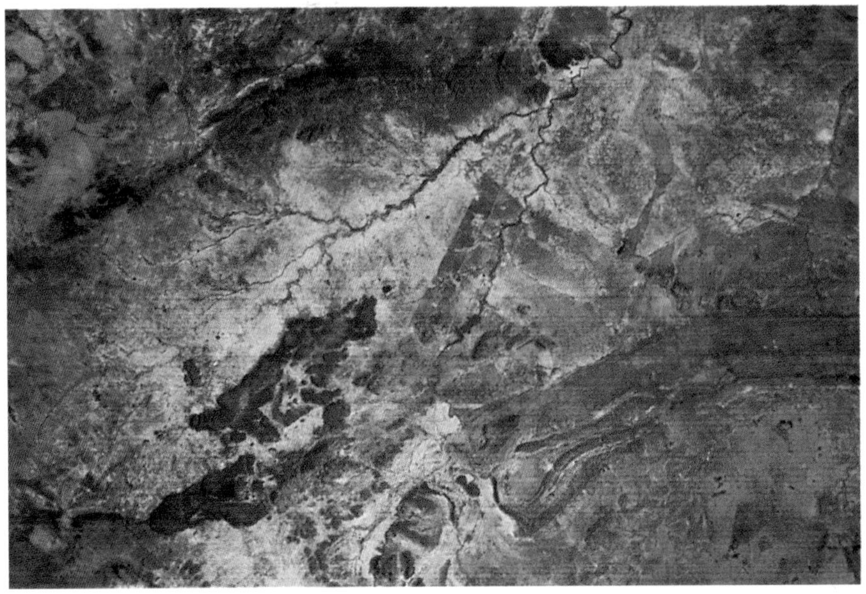

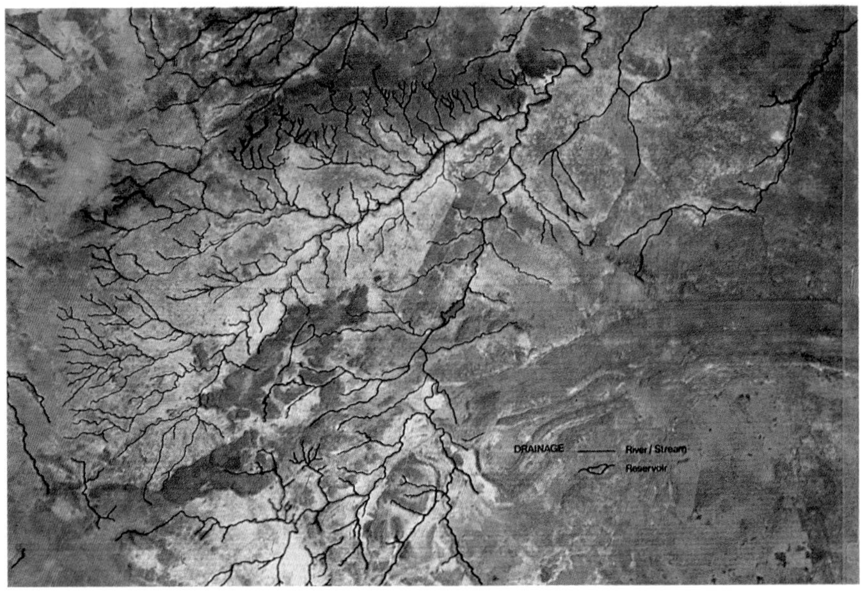

A study of 4,000km of roads to establish the order in which these roads should be upgraded. Satellite imagery was used to enable large areas with difficult access to be evaluated in a limited time.

The assessment of the cost effectiveness of an infra-red thermographic survey in identifying energy conservation opportunities and stimulating local community interest.

The lattice arch structure of the 1816 bridge over the River Wye was found to be considerably overstressed. Strengthening measures included unobtrusive new steel arches stressed into position whilst the bridge remained open to traffic.

The design of structure and services to accommodate a satellite station.

The 3,000m^2 walls and roof of the new laboratories are covered by PTFE coated-glass fabric membranes.

MOWLEM
MOWLEM

LEP TRANSPORT LTD
Lep

The light structure of polycarbonate pyramids and timber bars is easily demountable. An underfloor air-conditioning system controls the microclimate within the building.

A tourist facility close to Ayers Rock which includes tension fabric membranes to provide shade and create a translucent roof structure.

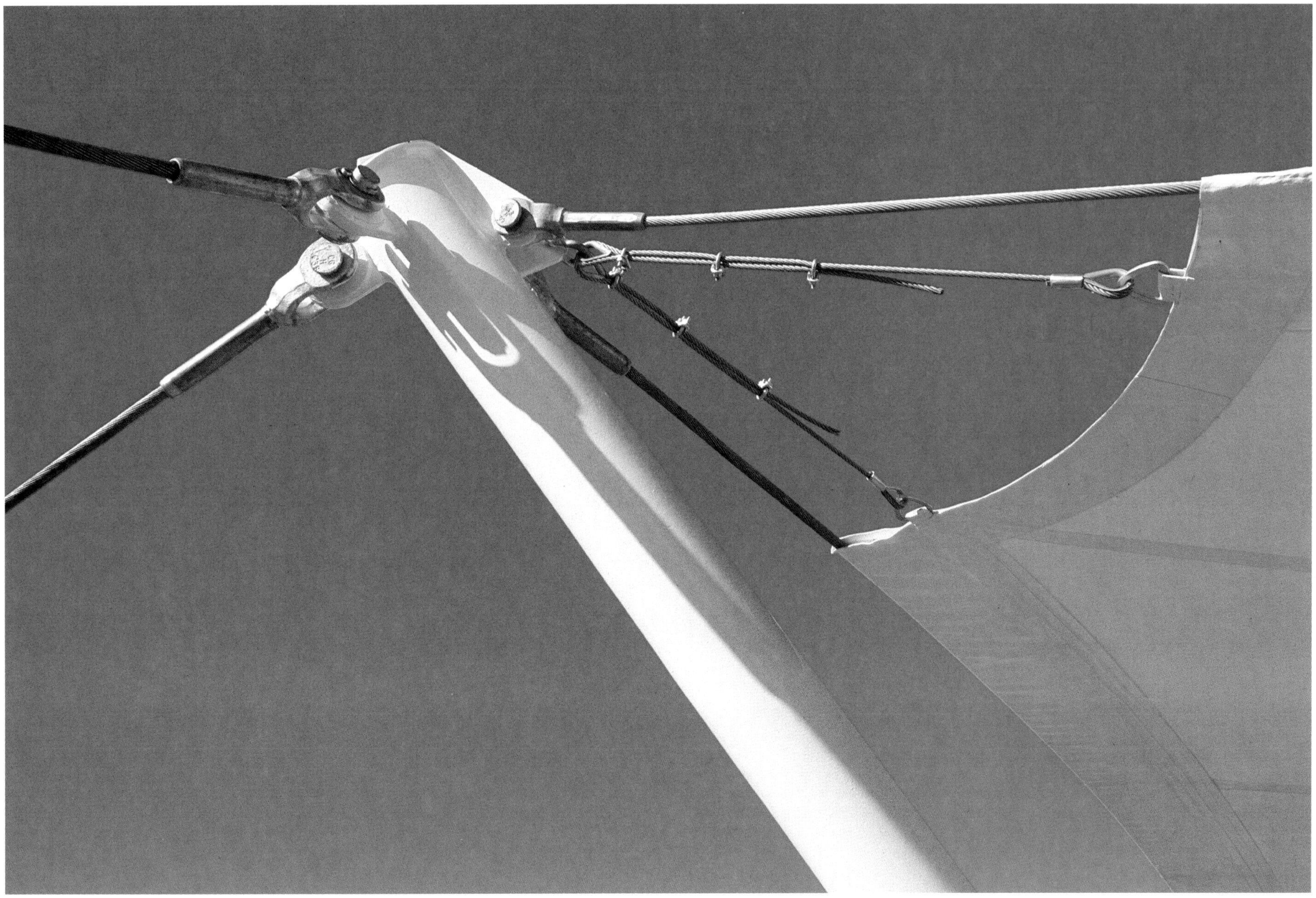

(0) milliseconds

50

100

Between 1981 and 1984 studies were carried out on severe accident hazards to flasks carrying irradiated nuclear power station fuel. These culminated in a public demonstration crash test in which a train travelling at 100 mph ran into a flask with only minimal damage to its exterior.

50

200

250

HILTON

Seawater Tunnel

ABANDONED LIMESTONE WORKINGS
West Midlands

Limestone mine caverns

Rock paste fill flowing into mine

Large quantities of limestone were mined in the West Midlands during the Industrial Revolution of the 18th and 19th centuries. Gradual collapse of the abandoned and unfilled workings caused surface subsidence. Remedial measures are in hand, including pumping rock paste made from colliery spoil into the cavities.

FESTIVAL HALL
Garden Festival, Stoke-on-Trent

CHRONOLOGY

1946 Practice founded by Ove Arup.
First Overseas Office established in Dublin.

1949 Ove Arup & Partners formed.
Ronald Jenkins, Geoffrey Wood, Andrew Young (res. 1951) taken into Partnership.

1955 First African Partnership formed in Nigeria.

1956 Peter Dunican taken into Partnership.

1957 First Regional Office established in Sheffield.

1960 First Scottish Office established in Edinburgh.

1961 Ronald Hobbs taken into Partnership.

1963 Irish Partnership formed.

1964 The Building Group of Ove Arup & Partners became Arup Associates.
Australian Partnership formed.

1965 Povl Ahm and Jack Zunz taken into Partnership

1966 Malaysian Partnership formed.

1967 UK Partnership name changed to Ove Arup & Partners Consulting Engineers.

1968 Fraser Anderson, Poul Beckmann, Frank Coffin, Philip Dowson, Ted Happold (res. 1976), Sid Heighway, Victor Kemp, John Martin, Tom Ridley, Bill Smyth, Derek Sugden, Malcolm Threlfall and Jack Waller appointed Executive Partners.

1969 Philip Dowson taken into Partnership.

1970 First Middle East Office established in Riyadh, Saudi Arabia.

First Welsh Office established in Cardiff.
Singapore Partnership formed.
Partners of Ove Arup & Partners became Partners in Ove Arup Partnership which became the Parent Firm of Ove Arup & Partners and Arup Associates.
Duncan Michael, Gordon Skepper (ret. 1985) and Werner Keis (res. 1977) appointed Executive Partners.

1972 Ronald Jenkins retired (dec. 1975).

1974 Michael Lewis appointed Executive Partner.

1976 Office established in Hong Kong.

1977 Geoffrey Wood retired and became Consultant.
Ove Arup & Partners, Ove Arup & Partners Scotland and Arup Associates were incorporated as companies with unlimited liability, all part of Ove Arup Partnership.
Peter Dunican became first Chairman of Ove Arup Partnership.
Directors of Ove Arup & Partners: Povl Ahm, Fraser Anderson (ret. 1984), Fred Butler (res. 1983), Ken Clayden, Frank Coffin (ret. 1985), Peter Dunican, Des Gurney, Sid Heighway (ret. 1980), David Henkel (ret. 1985), Basil Isaacs, Victor Kemp, Michael Lewis, John Martin, Duncan Michael, Jorgen Nissen, Tom Ridley, Ken Shaw, Malcolm Simpson, Bill Smyth, Malcolm Threlfall, Nigel Thompson, Jack Zunz (Chairman).

Directors of Ove Arup & Partners Scotland: Brian Baxter, Sandy Fraser, Jim Hampson, Duncan Michael, Jorgen Nissen, Tom Ridley (Chairman), Hamish Stears, Bryan Wright (res. 1979).

Brunei and Sabah Partnerships formed.

1978 Peter Rice appointed Director of Ove Arup & Partners.

1979 Tom Barker, Bob Emmerson, Richard Haryott, Jim Hampson, Ernie Irwin, Michael Shears, John Sinnett (res. 1985) appointed Directors of Ove Arup & Partners.

1980 Jim Morrish appointed Director of Ove Arup & Partners.

1982 Michael Sargent, Martyn Stroud appointed Directors of Ove Arup & Partners.

1983 Brian Baxter, Roy Cowap, David Croft, Sandy Fraser and David Johnston appointed Directors of Ove Arup & Partners.

1984 Ronald Hobbs and Jack Zunz became Co-Chairmen of Ove Arup Partnership.
Povl Ahm became Chairman of Ove Arup & Partners.

1985 Derek Ball, Cecil Balmond, Alan Foster, Mike Glover, David Gordon, Alan Hughes, Keith Law, Iain Lyall, Martin Manning, John C Miles, Ian Mudd, John Pilkington, Brian Simpson and Tony Stevens became Directors of Ove Arup & Partners.

Peter Dunican retired from the Board and became Consultant.

1986 Jim Hampson became Chairman of Ove Arup & Partners Scotland.
David Whittleton appointed a Director of Ove Arup & Partners.
Derek Blackwood and David Colley appointed Directors of Ove Arup & Partners Scotland.

Detail of Dome Girder, Rubber Factory, Brynmawr.

PROJECTS

KEY TO SERVICES
Principal services provided for the realisation of projects illustrated in the book are:

- BC Business Communications
- BE Building Engineering (All engineering disciplines required for the design of buildings)
- C Civil Engineering (Highways, Bridges, Airports, Coastal, Transportation, Geotechnics)
- CC Cost Control
- E Economics
- ES Energy Surveys
- IT Information Technology
- M&E Mechanical & Electrical
- PA Prime Agency
- PM Project Management
- PP Project Planning
- S Structural Engineering
- SE Specialist Engineering Consultancy
- T Transportation
- TA Technical Agents
- TAE Technical Assessment & Evaluation
- TL Telecommunications
- TM Technical Management

Other specialist services provided include: Acoustics; Computer Graphics; Cost Engineering; Environmental Physics; Environmental Wind Analysis; Fire Engineering; Materials Technology; Smoke Movement Analysis; Structural Pathology; Systems Engineering.

TITLE	CLIENT	ARCHITECT	SERVICE
Penguin Pool Zoological Gardens, London	The Zoological Society of London	Lubetkin & Tecton	S
Highpoint Highgate, London	Gestetner Ltd. with Northfield (Highgate) Ltd.	Lubetkin & Tecton	S
Arcon Mark V Demountable House	Ministry of Public Buildings & Works	Arcon Ltd. Architect: A.M. Gear	S
Rosebery Avenue Flats London	Finsbury Borough Council	Lubetkin & Tecton	S
Bus Station Dublin	Coras Iompair Eireann	Michael Scott	S
Rubber Factory Brynmawr, Wales	Enfield Cables Ltd.	Architects Co-Partnership	S
Footbridge Festival of Britain, London	Festival of Britain Authority		PA
Aero Research Duxford, Cambridgeshire	Aero Research Ltd.		PA
Hangars RAF Gaydon	John Laing & Son for the Air Ministry		S
Hunstanton Secondary Modern School Norfolk	Norfolk County Council	Alison & Peter Smithson	S
Mayfield School Putney, London	London County Council	Powell & Moya	S

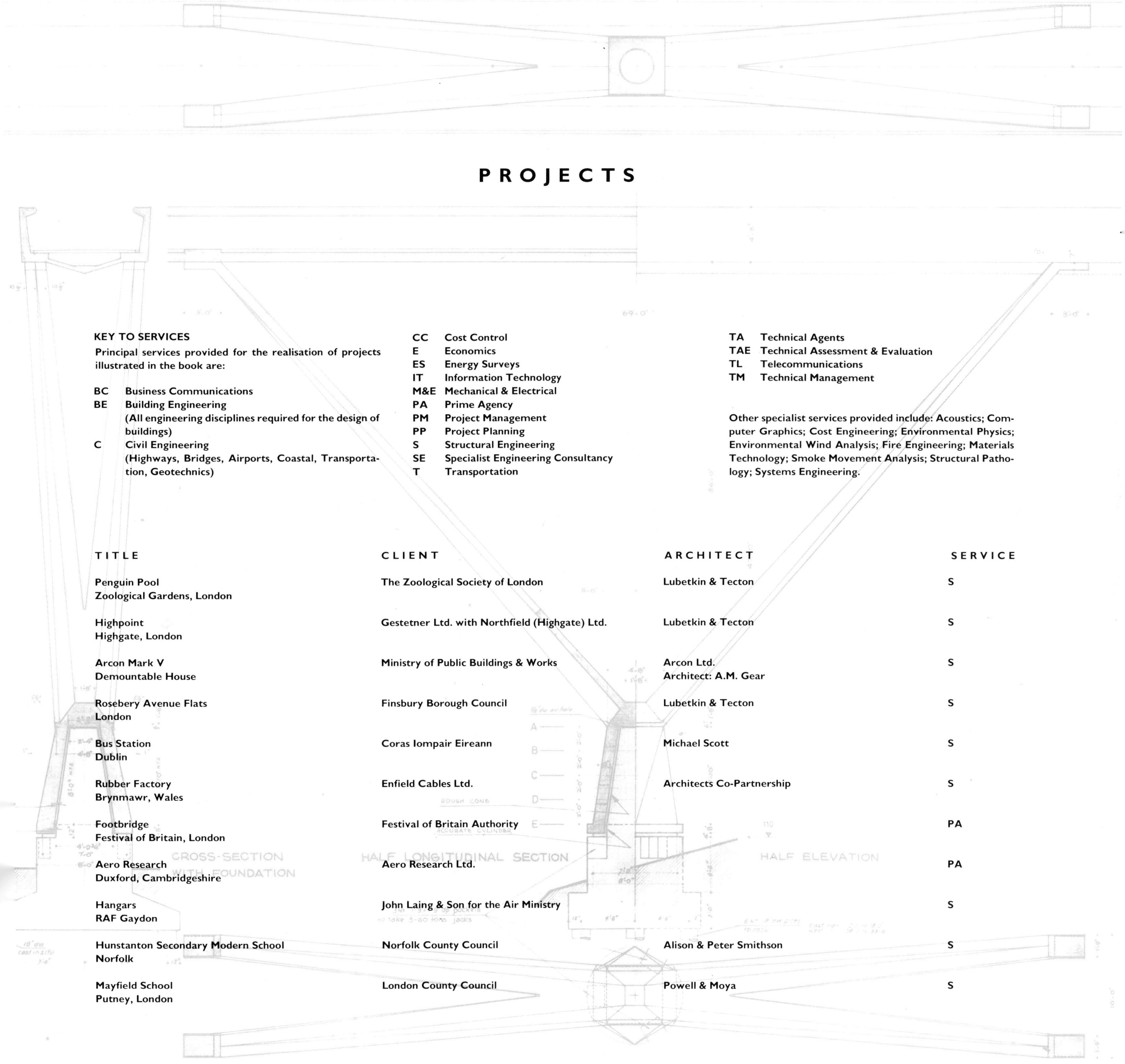

Kingsgate Footbridge, Durham University.

TITLE	CLIENT	ARCHITECT	SERVICE
Bank of England Printing Works Debden, Essex	Bank of England	Easton & Robertson	S
Workshop Block Cement and Concrete Association Wexham Springs, Buckinghamshire	Cement and Concrete Association	W.G. Oram, Association Architect	S
Alton Estate Roehampton, London	London County Council	Architect to the Council	S
Trades Union Congress Memorial Building London	Trades Union Congress	David Du R. Aberdeen & Partners	S
Hangars, Air Support Command Abingdon	John Laing & Son for the Air Ministry		S
Princess Margaret Hospital Swindon, Wiltshire	Oxford Regional Hospital Board	Powell & Moya	S
Park Hill Housing Sheffield, Yorkshire	Sheffield City Corporation	Sheffield City Architect	S
Telecommunications Tower Johannesburg	South African Broadcasting Corporation	South African Broadcasting Corporation	PM, C, S
Telecommunications Tower Johannesburg	South African Department of Public Works for the Department of Post & Telephones	Department of Public Works	PM, C, S
Andrews Boathouse Eton College	Eton College	Michael Patrick	PM, S
26 St James's Place London	Malvin Investment Co. Ltd.	Denys Lasdun & Partners	S
Coventry Cathedral	Coventry Cathedral Reconstruction Committee	Sir Basil Spence OM RA	S
University and Teaching Hospital Ibadan, Nigeria	Nigerian Public Works Department	W.H. Watkins Gray & Partners	S
Mulago Hospital Kampala, Uganda	The Government of Uganda	Architect to the Government	S
Smithfield Market London	Corporation of the City of London	T.P. Bennett & Son	S
Independence House Lagos, Nigeria	Federal Ministry of Works & Housing	Federal Ministry of Works & Housing	C, S
Kingsgate Footbridge Durham University	Durham University		PA
Dunelm House Durham University	Durham University	Architects Co-Partnership	S
National Recreation Centre Crystal Palace, London	London County Council for the Central Council for Physical Recreation	Architect to the Council	C, S
Hampstead Civic Centre London	Hampstead Borough Council	Sir Basil Spence, Bonnington & Collins	S
St Catherine's College Oxford University	Oxford University	Professor Arne Jacobsen	S
Ninewells Hospital Dundee, Scotland	Eastern Region Hospital Board	Robert Matthew, Johnson-Marshall & Partners	S
Fairydean Football Club Stand Galashiels, Scotland	Fairydean Football Club	Peter Womersley	S

Stadium Canopy, National Recreation Centre, Crystal Palace.

TITLE	CLIENT	ARCHITECT	SERVICE
Royal College of Physicians London	Royal College of Physicians	Denys Lasdun & Partners	S
Law Library Oxford University	Oxford University	Sir Leslie Martin in association with Colin St John Wilson	S
Ahmadu Bello Stadium Kaduna, Nigeria	Northern Region Government	Fry, Drew & Atkinson	C, S
Cocoa Storage Sheds Lagos, Nigeria	Western Region Marketing Board	Design Group, Nigeria	S
Assembly Hall Bootham School, York	Bootham School	Trevor Dannatt	S
International Students Hostel Sussex Gardens, London	International Students Club (Church of England) Ltd.	Farrell Grimshaw Partnership	S
Hangars Lusaka, Zambia	Government of Zambia		PA
Volta River Bridges Ghana	Ghana National Construction Corporation		PA
Sapele Bridges Nigeria	Western State Government		PA
Terminal Building Abbotsinch Airport, Glasgow	Glasgow City Council	Sir Basil Spence, Glover & Ferguson	C, S
Library Edinburgh University	Edinburgh University	Sir Basil Spence, Glover & Ferguson	C, S
Queen Elizabeth Hall and Hayward Gallery, London	London County Council	Architect to the Council	S
Radio Aerial County Police Headquarters, Durham	Durham County Police Authority		PA
Sunderland Civic Centre	Corporation of Sunderland	Sir Basil Spence, Bonnington & Collins	S
Sussex University	Sussex University	Sir Basil Spence, Bonnington & Collins	S
Residences University of East Anglia, Norwich	University of East Anglia	Denys Lasdun & Partners	S
The Standard Bank Johannesburg	The Standard Bank Ltd.	Hentrich, Petschnigg & Partners in association with Professor E.W.N. Mallows. Executive Architects: Stucke Harrison Ritchie & Partners	S
Royal Commonwealth Pool Edinburgh	Corporation of Edinburgh	Robert Matthew, Johnson-Marshall & Partners	S
Western Bank Bridge and Concourse Sheffield University	Sheffield University		PA
West African Roads	State and National Governments		PA
Perak Turf Club Grandstand Ipoh, Malaysia	Perak Turf Club	Joyce Nankivell Associates	S
Raising and Refurbishing The Wellington Inn Market Place, Manchester	Central & District Properties Ltd. Refurbishment: Bass Charrington Ltd.	Cruickshank & Seward Refurbishment: F.W.B. Charles	C, S
Gateshead Highway	Gateshead Metropolitan Borough Council		PA
Gateshead Western By-Pass	Durham County and Gateshead Borough Councils		PA

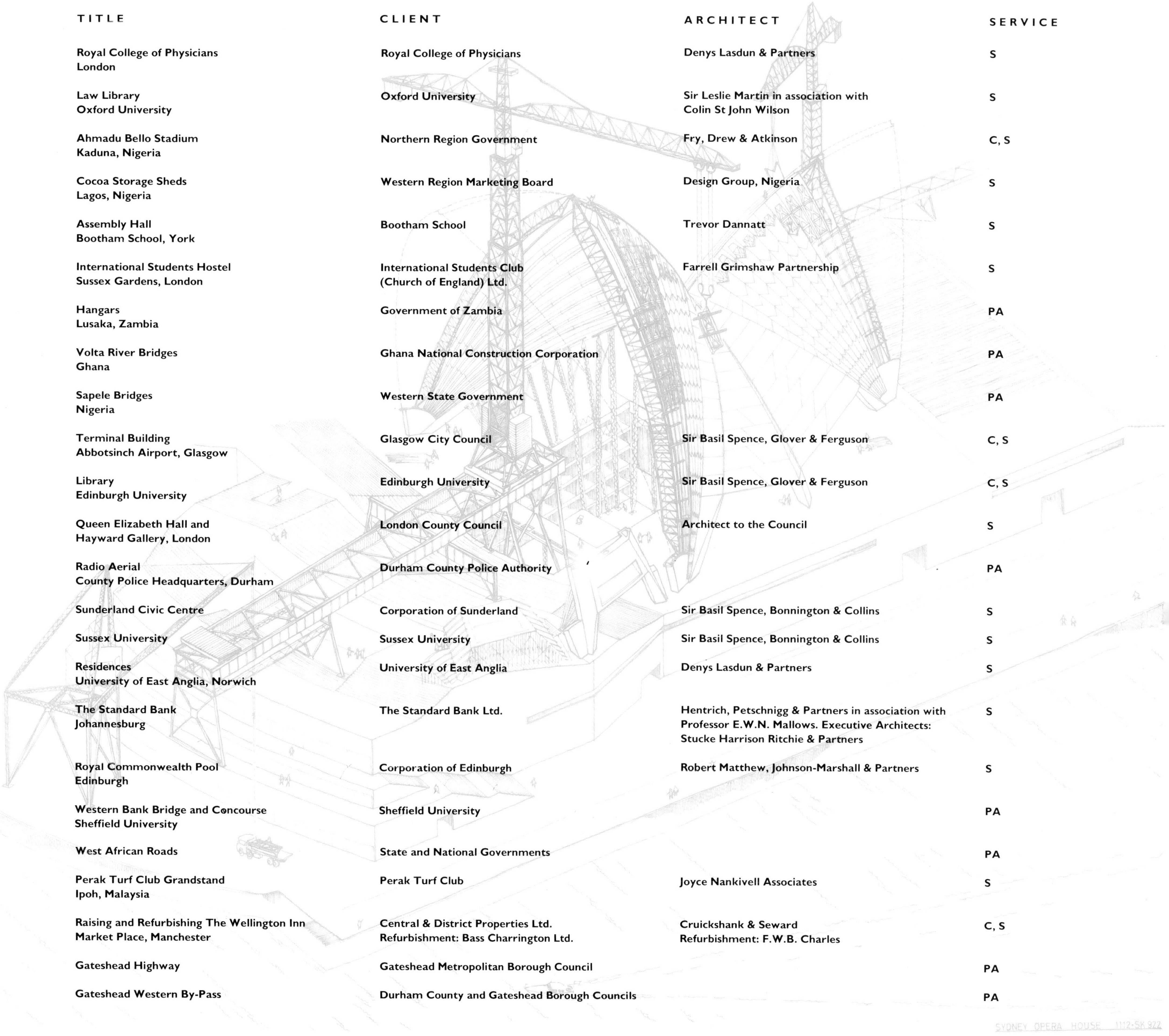

Construction Isometric, Sydney Opera House, Australia.

TITLE	CLIENT	ARCHITECT	SERVICE
British Embassy Rome	Directorate of Estate Management, Overseas Department of the Environment	Sir Basil Spence OM RA	S
Crucible Theatre Sheffield	Sheffield Playhouse	Renton Howard Wood & Partners	S
Emley Moor Television Tower Yorkshire	Independent Broadcasting Authority		PA
The Stock Exchange London	Stock Exchange (London) Holdings Ltd.	Llewelyn-Davies, Weeks, Forestier-Walker & Bor in association with Fitzroy Robinson & Partners	S
Almondell Footbridge Scotland	Midlothian County Council	Morris Steadman	PM, S
Bernat Klein Studio High Sunderland, Scotland	Bernat Klein Studio	Peter Womersley	S
York Minster Structural Restoration	The Dean and Chapter of York Minster	Bernard M. Feilden, Surveyor to the Fabric	C, S
Carlsberg Brewery Northampton	Carlsberg Breweries Ltd.	Knud Munk	CC, BE
National Stadium Lagos, Nigeria	Federal Government of Nigeria	Mence Moore & Mort	C, S
Extension to Keble College Oxford University	Keble College, Oxford University	Ahrends Burton & Koralek	S
Northwick Park Hospital Harrow, Middlesex	North-Western Regional Hospital Board and the Medical Research Council	Llewelyn-Davies, Weeks, Forestier-Walker & Bor	S
Society of Friends Meeting House Blackheath, London	Society of Friends	Trevor Dannatt	S
Hotel and Conference Centre Riyadh, Saudi Arabia	Ministry of Finance, Government of the Kingdom of Saudi Arabia	Trevor Dannatt	S
Habitat Warehouse, Showrooms and Offices Wallingford	Ryman Conran Ltd.	Ahrends Burton & Koralek	BE
Federal Garden Show Mannheim, West Germany	City of Mannheim	Büro Mutschler & Partners Roof Consultant: Professor Frei Otto	S
Hotel and Conference Centre Mecca, Saudi Arabia	Ministry of Finance, Government of the Kingdom of Saudi Arabia	Professor Frei Otto and Rolf Gutbrod	S
Bishopthorpe Bridge York	Department of Transport		PA
Jerangau-Jabor Road Malaysia	Malaysian Ministry of Public Works		PA
Microwave Towers	GEC Telecommunications & Others		PA
Birmingham Civic Centre	Birmingham City Council	John Madin Design Group in association with the City Architect	C, S
Scottish Widows' Headquarters Offices Edinburgh	Scottish Widows' Fund & Life Assurance Society	Sir Basil Spence, Glover & Ferguson	S
Richmond Recreation Centre North Yorkshire	Richmond District Council	Napper, Errington, Collerton Partnership	S
Berry Lane Viaduct, M25 Hertfordshire	Department of Transport		PA

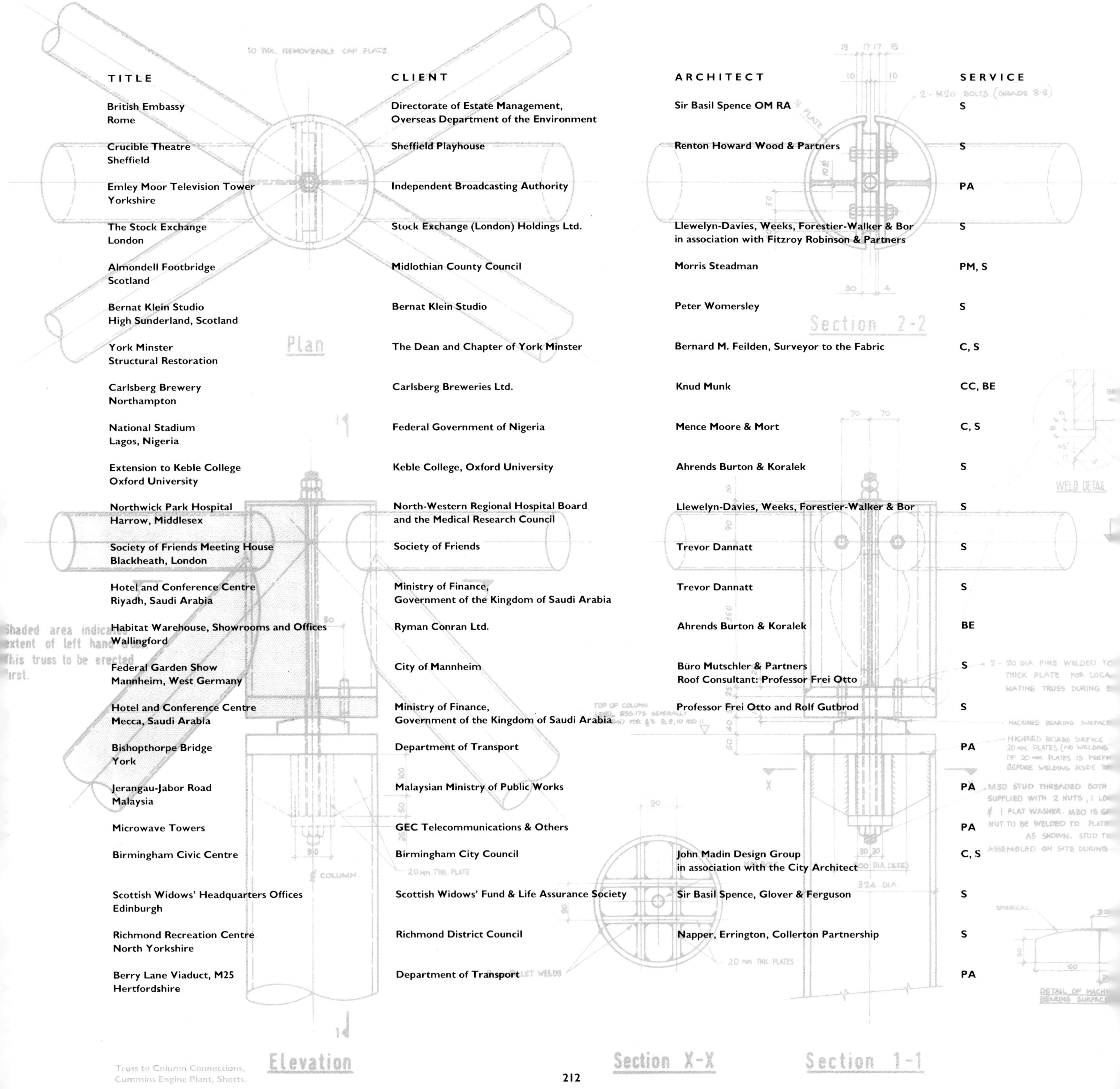

Truss to Column Connections,
Cummins Engine Plant, Shotts.

TITLE	CLIENT	ARCHITECT	SERVICE
Sydney Opera House Australia	Government of New South Wales	Stages 1 & 2: Jørn Utzon Stage 3: Hall Todd & Littlemore	PM, C, S
Centre Culturel Georges Pompidou Paris	Etablissement Public du Centre Pompidou	Piano & Rogers	PP, BE
Royal Exchange Theatre Manchester	Theatre 69	Levitt Bernstein Associates	S
OCBC Centre Singapore	Overseas Chinese Banking Corporation	I.M. Pei & Partners (New York) in conjunction with BEP Akitek (Singapore)	S
Siak River Bridge Sumatra, Indonesia	P.T. Leightons (Indonesia) Construction Co. Ltd.		PA
Library St Andrews University,	St Andrews University	Faulkner-Brown, Hendy, Watkinson, Stonor	S
Arts Building Trinity College, Dublin	Trinity College, Dublin	Ahrends, Burton & Koralek	S
Runnymede Bridge, M25 Staines	Department of Transport	Consultant: Arup Associates	PA
Byker Viaduct Tyne & Wear Metro	Tyne & Wear Passenger Transport Executive	Consultant: Renton Howard Wood Levin Partnership	PA
Queensferry Interchange Flintshire, Wales	The Welsh Office		PA
Brighton Marina, Sussex (All structures within sea wall, access roads and ramps)	Brighton Marina Co. Ltd.	The Louis de Soissons Partnership	C, S
St Katharine Dock Redevelopment London	Port of London Authority	Renton Howard Wood & Partners	C, S
Hopewell Centre Hong Kong	Hopewell Holdings, Hong Kong	Gordon Wu & Associates	C, S
Brent C. Flare Tower North Sea	Shell UK Exploration & Production Ltd.		SE
Hutton Tension Leg Platform	Conoco (UK) Ltd.		SE, TM
National Exhibition Centre Birmingham	The National Exhibition Centre Ltd.	Site Planning & External Works: R. Seifert & Partners. Buildings: Edward D. Mills & Partners	C, BE
Restoration of Theatre Royal Nottingham	Nottingham City Council	Renton Howard Wood Levin Partnership	S
Nottingham Concert Hall	Nottingham City Council	Renton Howard Wood Levin Partnership	BE
Auld Brig O'Doon Strathclyde, Scotland	Kyle & Carrick District Council		C
Robinson College Cambridge University	Trustees of Robinson College	Gillespie Kidd & Coia in conjunction with YRM	S
Prince Philip Dental Teaching Hospital Hong Kong	Architectural Office of Public Works Department Hong Kong	YRM International	BE
Carlsberg Brewery Hong Kong	United Brewery Ltd.	Consultant: Anders Helsted (APS) Copenhagen YRM International	PA
Amersham International Cardiff	Amersham International Ltd.	Percy Thomas Partnership	S

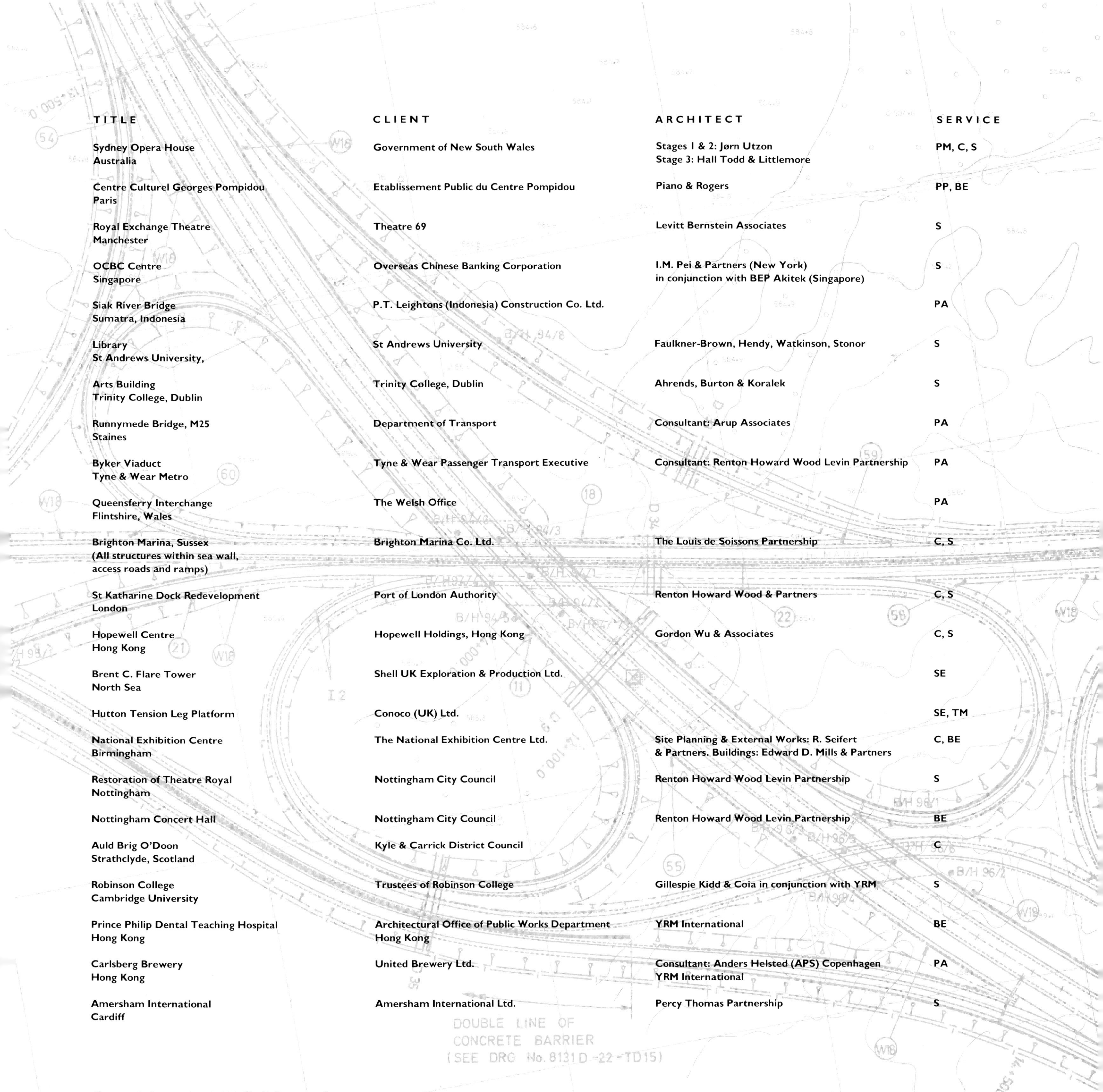

Thumamah Intersection, Jeddah-Riyadh-Dammam Expressway, Saudi Arabia.

TITLE	CLIENT	ARCHITECT	SERVICE
Ashley Centre Epsom, Surrey	Ashley Avenue Development Ltd. for the Borough of Epsom and Ewell and Friends Provident Life Office	Renton Howard Wood Levin Partnership	BE
The Friary Centre Guildford, Surrey	MEPC plc	Sidney Kaye Firmin Partnership	S
Fleetguard Factory and Distribution Centre Quimper, France	Ville de Quimper and Fleetguard International Corporation	Richard Rogers & Partners	BE
The Barbican Development London	Corporation of the City of London	Chamberlin Powell & Bon	C, S
Cummins Engine Plant Shotts, Scotland	Cummins Engine Co. Ltd.	Ahrends, Burton & Koralek	BE
Extension, Doha Power Station Kuwait	International Contracting Co., Kuwait, for the Ministry of Electricity & Water, Kuwait		PA
Berrima Cement Works Expansion New South Wales, Australia	Blue Circle Southern Cement Ltd.	Consultant: Peter Hall	C, S
Derngate Theatre Northampton	Northampton Borough Council	Renton Howard Wood Levin Partnership	BE
Thames Tunnel Mills Housing Rotherhithe, London	London & Quadrant Housing Trust	Hunt Thompson Associates	BE
Allendale Square Perth, Australia	Allendale Properties Pty. Ltd.	Cameron Chisholm & Nicol	S
Articulated Loading Column Maureen Field, North Sea	Entreprise d'Equipements Mécaniques et Hydrauliques (EMH), for Phillips Petroleum Co.		SE
Mass Transit Railway, Hong Kong Tsuen Wan Depot, Luk Yeung Sun Chuen Development	Mass Transit Railway Corporation. Developer: Luk Yeung Sun Chuen. Joint venture	For Depot: Tao Ho Design Architects For Estate: Choa Ko & Partners in association with Lee & Zee Associates	BE S
Old Vic Theatre Refurbishment London	Old Vic Theatre	Renton Howard Wood Levin Partnership	BE
Theatre Royal Plymouth	Plymouth City Council	Peter Moro Partnership	BE
St John Boste Church Washington, Tyne & Wear	The Parish of St John Boste	Napper Collerton Partnership	S
Triton Court London	Royal London Mutual Assurance Society Ltd.	Sheppard Robson	BE
Renault Centre Swindon, Wiltshire	Renault UK Ltd.	Foster Associates	BE
Kylesku Bridge Scotland	Highland Regional Council		PA
Staatsgalerie Stuttgart, West Germany	LAND Baden-Württemburg	James Stirling & Partners	BE
Patscenter Princeton, USA	PA International Management Consultants Ltd.	Richard Rogers & Partners	BE
Canopy Roof and Supports, Hummingbird Theatre Zoological Society of London	Bovis Coverspan Ltd. for Zoological Society of London	John Toovey, Architect to the Society	S
New Grandstand, Lansdowne Road Dublin	Irish Rugby Football Union		PA

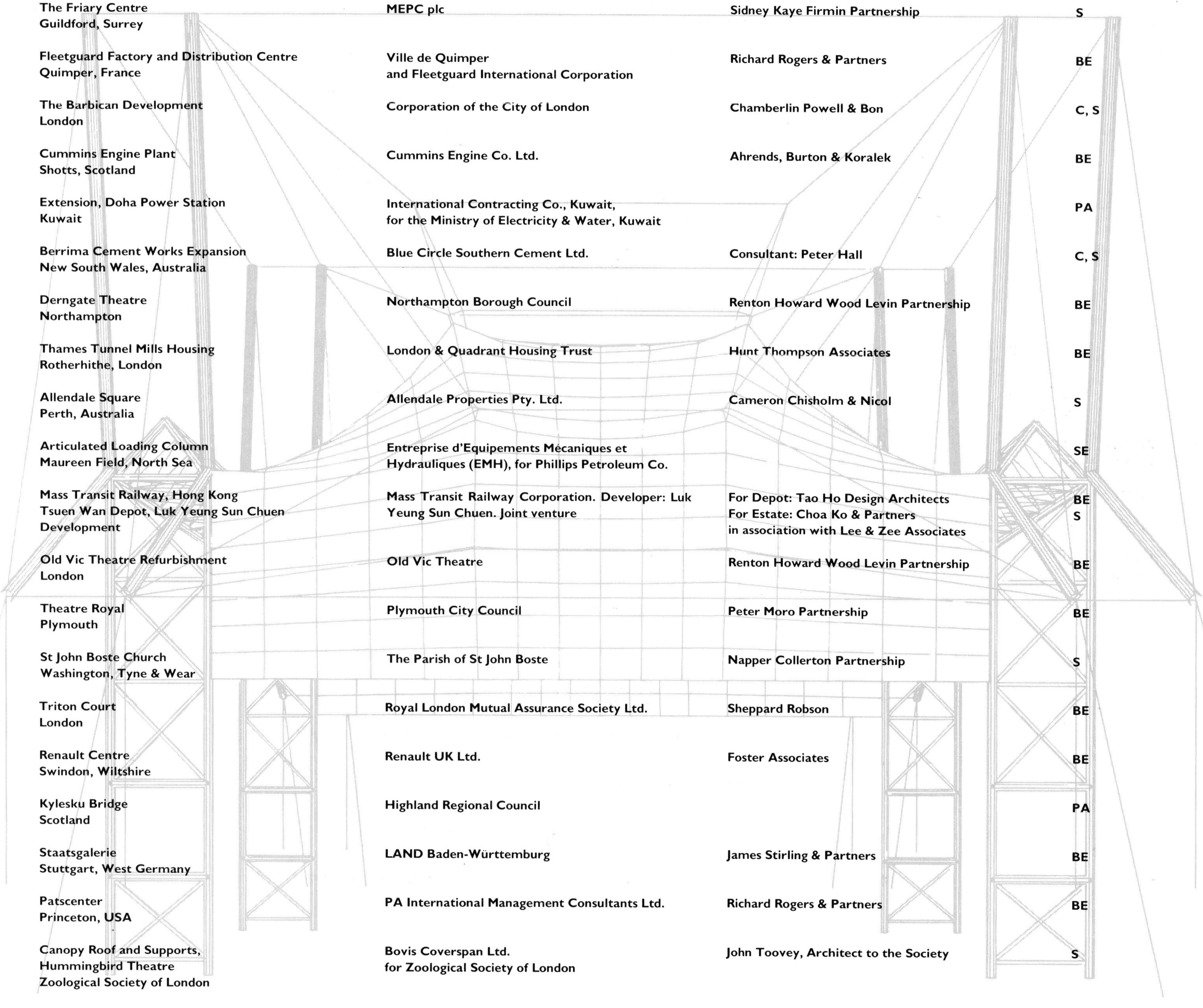

Computer Plot, Schlumberger Fabric Roof, Cambridge.